CW00862949

A Book For Pandora

A Book For Pandora

Kathryn Rossati

Copyright (C) 2019 Kathryn Rossati

Layout design and Copyright (C) 2019 by Next Chapter

Published 2019 by Magnum Opus – A Next Chapter Imprint

Cover art by Cover Mint

This book is a work of fiction. Names, characters, places, and incidents are the product of the author's imagination or are used fictitiously. Any resemblance to actual events, locales, or persons, living or dead, is purely coincidental.

All rights reserved. No part of this book may be reproduced or transmitted in any form or by any means, electronic or mechanical, including photocopying, recording, or by any information storage and retrieval system, without the author's permission.

www.kathrynrossati.co.uk

Contents

Part One: Shadow Dance

The Vision

As the weightless wings brush my face,
fluttering against my vision,
I feel the path open up again.
A shallow wave licks my ankles
and fills the rock pools
with miniature lifeforms
that have no idea I'm here.
Like full lips parting
the wave draws back.
My feet follow,
ignoring the jagged rocks
that threaten to pierce the skin.
In the distance,
I see the family beckon to me,
holding out their hands for me to grasp.
But I'm bodiless,
my grip lost
to the horizon.
Once again,
I must turn away.

Our Sweet Fortress

We build up walls
to hide our little cocoon
of love,
with bright threads
woven into a snug blanket
and a casing of polished ebony.
The heat of the sun warms us
as time passes,
grasses grow up around us
and wildflowers bloom year after year.
Our hands are constantly entwined,
and will be
until they are hands no more.

The Demise of a Splash of Green in an Otherwise Grey World

The hard droplets pound
away at the pavement;
the dainty daisies growing in the cracks
stand no chance
against this sudden onslaught.
They fall flat,
squashed not only by the weight of the rain,
but crunched by wheels and feet,
all rushing past as though
they
are the ones
whose petals
are being washed
into the dark drain.

The River Guards

A gathering of columns,
decorated with bright, orange blooms
that cascade their scent
on the decayed air,
stand bold against the grey river.
To them,
Satan is just a song
that drifts down on the wind,
but for those who sail,
unwillingly,
beyond the columns' reach,
the song is more
a delighted warning of what awaits,
hellishly reminiscent
of the jaw-jarring scraping
of human fingernails on a blackboard,
drawn so fiercely across
that the nails are ripped away
from the cuticles.
The song instils anxiety into every
body.
What kind of creature
could possibly make such
a sound?

Propaganda

Red sweeps across the heavily veined
fingers clutching tightly
at the bulbous purple node;
a ruby mass fails to plug the seam
that widens with each breath.
The stain soaks deep
into the carpet fibres,
already building its resistance to being cleaned.
A perpetual reminder,
unless covered by a rug
so full of patterns that the looker
feels nauseated if their gaze lingers.
But, of course,
even so garish a distraction
is preferable to the plans
lurking beneath it.
So they say.

Mother-in-law's Tongue

Forked, flecked like an
open mouth covered in spittle
in the midst
of an argument.
It sits in the shade,
biding its time,
watching for the perfect moment.
A suggestion here,
a remark there,
growing and growing
like a green, coiled snake
guarding every movement,
day and night.

Onwards to the Rotting Tiles

The chess piece is split down the middle,
parading as two - in a mirror you can see
it whole, moving puppet-stringed
across the board, never waiting for a second
to consider the effect having the image
of an extra player has on the other pawns.
One side is stained black, the other bleached,
but what of the grey space in between?
Sticky, sap-covered moss disguises it;
no-one can see that inside they are the same.

Gloop

It all started on
a Monday;
the contents of the pot dribbled
onto the floor,
flooding the newly polished tiles
with a voluminous
dark gloop.

The gloop was a mistake,
a recipe
gone wrong
from the mass of ingredients
forced to boil together.
Just like her life.
Spread out so thin
that she was barely a droplet of herself.

Working through the week,
she swept up the gloop
into heavy-duty sacks and buried it
among the mountains
of other people's waste.

But for years after,
the gloop's dark stain
remained.

Soiled Glass

The chugging of the engine wakes me;
I am tainted
with its fumes.
A blackened face
in a blackened mirror,
a copy made of carbon
filled with the discards of personality.

My doppelganger's stupidity
faces me every day,
always solid with the expression of the trapped.

Ironic, don't you think?

If only I could roll it up
into little balls of doughy flesh
and pop them into my mouth one by one,
chewing and chewing until the juices
flow out
and I can use them to wipe away
the layers of coal-dusted
skin.

Cubed

Inside the neat black cube
lies a silver heart.
It has never felt the breath of air
that comes from an open box.

For all its years,
the metal is worn
only slightly;
if it were of flora,
then it would be as green
as the newest seedling
and have experienced
even less.

A sudden jolt
jars the black cube.
It falls from its perch
down
to the floor.
The heart doesn't know
what to do.
Its world is changing.
The cube is broken;
air and light finally leak in.

The Neat Gurney

A glimmer catches your eye,
you look closer, taking in
the brightness and separating it
from the image beyond.
There you see her eyes sparkling
blue, full of hope
that tugs at your being.
You dare to believe her optimism
is not misguided,
but then the mirror darkens,
clouded by a storm of muttering.
The doctor says this is normal.
Still, deep down,
you can't help but fear
the worst.

Gift-wrapped

From the dovecote the song
drifts down.
I pause my binding,
cocking my head to listen:
something about it is familiar, but not,
like the aftertaste of a bitter fruit
you only half-remember eating.
I carry on, threading
the thin, gold cords
together.
This soul's organs
can't escape.

Beyond the Naked Eye

Yours is the shaded bench placed beside the stream where tired walkers rest their feet whilst watching the ducks at play.

Yours is the mansion with the ivy climbing high to the window of the first floor bedroom, where its creeping tendrils lightly finger the latch.

Yours is the garden that is home to upright stones marked with old names, beaten down by wind and rain to become unreadable.

And yours is the oak tree that has been growing for a thousand years, whose roots intertwine with the forgotten skulls in the invisible pit.

A Cool Cup of Ink

Darkness leans against my heart
readying itself to start
synchronizing with every beat
and drinking in the soft heat.

I climb the walls again
writhing inwardly from the pain,
losing sleep yet never awake,
a curse that I can never break.

The Shackles That Have No Key

I hunt the moon
as it searches the sandy shores,
looking for the key it will never find.
My licking flames
touch its hide,
illuminating it for all the world to see,
but so lost
in its task is it
that the heat worries it not.
With a whine of despair that only hints
at the true longing
in its crater-flecked heart,
it extends its gentle, pale
hands down to tug at the ocean,
pulling the waves back like blankets
cast from a bed.
Come now, my friend,
I cannot remove your shackles,
but I can take you from them.

I Am

I am invisible,
but you are so solid
even your thoughts are
impenetrable.

I am endangered,
yet your species has
flourished to the point
where resources are scarce.

My home is shrinking,
but yours now takes over
every continent, even encroaching
on mine.

We are dying,
and so are you, but you hide
that fact from each other,
pretending it *isn't real.*

Playing Cards

I search through the deck of cards, upsetting the neatness of the stack. It doesn't matter, I can tidy them later; line them up and place them all in order, making sure everything is correct, that the story still flows.

Out of line is the only way I can see the stats clearly, see my qualities measured against each other.

Can I really call them qualities?

I don't know, but at least I have proof that they exist. That I exist. Until my small house of cards tumbles to the floor.

Life Lines

I keep it locked away in a small box
I paint it on my skin
I wear it in my smile
I hide it in a bottle of gin.
I hold it out like a banner
I tuck it in my boots
I coat it in beeswax
I simply don't give two hoots.
I display it proud on a shelf
I hug it tight to my chest
I watch it and make notes
I take pleasure in giving it out as a test.

The Feasting of the Pitcher

Dive into my belly,
you quick-footed buzzing fool.
Let me trap you
among my garden of dead.
No more flitting from
place to place, never
content to rest for more than a day.
Leaving only trails of disease
behind, why would they ever appreciate you?
Let me drown you,
so that your dull hum is finally
silenced.
No-one will mourn you,
but I promise to stand forever
as your monument.

Part Two: Sweet Scents

A Rainy Afternoon

It begins as a light tapping
on glass,
a rhythmic patter
of ghostly fingers
that leave only tear streaks down the pane.
Wellies left outside the door
in a rush
soon begin to fill
and seeds cast on bird tables glisten
like small nuggets of gold.
The smell of the earth rises,
bringing forth a crowd of slugs and snails
who rummage through fallen leaves.
A tiny river courses along the path,
wetting moss and stone,
finally pooling in the dip that always stays
just a little bit damp.

That In Between Place

The cogs grind against
mushy cloud,
stirring the fluff into shape:
a solid form of wakefulness
that yearns to drift apart.
Bind it tight,
coil the springs up
with a stern twist of key;
barricade it against the cushy strands.
Tick. Tick. Tick.
Tock.
The alarm sings its unwelcome greeting.

On the Move

Rolling hills tumble;
the train passes them before a breath can be taken.
No chugging along,
full
speed
ahead!

Gazes dip as it reaches the bridge.
The earth falls away.

We are floating. Momentarily.

Swift as a swift,
the ground stacks itself again.
Exhales are heard -
the hills give a thundering chuckle.

Ripples

A ripple in a glass of water
can never leave the glass.
Yet if the glass ever cracks,
the water can push against it,
working away to force an opening.
Even if the gap it makes is only
wide enough for a trickle to escape,
sometimes that trickle is all that's needed.
Seeping across the table,
weaving its way through discarded cutlery,
crusted salt and pepper pots
and past dusty, fine china plates
to the edge, where droplets form
ready to drip into the dry soil
filling the plant pot below.
The fresh seeds lying in wait
beneath the surface
will finally get
their spark of life.

The Eager and the Patient

When the door opens
Out bounds
The bumbling bundle of bouncing energy
Wagging its tail
With flaming, eager, sightless eyes.
Uncontrollable happy smiles
Brim from its jowls
Demanding cuddles.

Behind, the experienced one sits
Keen gaze fixed on the attention
The blind bundle receives.
Foolish. Untrained. Impulsive.
But sometimes worth indulging
In a game of tug o' war.
Part of the family now,
After all.

Circular Breathing

A spinning top spins
on the edge of a cliff,
gradually wearing away the chalk.
As the last bit crumbles,
the top falls, plunging
at such a speed
that it doesn't have a chance to stop
rotating.
On its way down,
it disturbs the breeze and sucks it in,
tasting all the places the air
has travelled,
knowing that the particles
are much more than just
what they are.
Then the top hits the water,
and the knowledge is gone.

Mind the Wallpaper

Every day I write a line on a sheet of paper,
and put it up on my wall.
They overlap,
white scales with tangles of black moss,
thick like fur and with plenty of space
between the layers
for dust and insects to collect,
just to let me know that clinging
on to old things
results in an unpleasant experience every time.
So if I can, I leave the lines alone -
there to look at in times of desperation
for inspiration
but never to be touched.
The lines aren't pretty.
They aren't ugly, either.
They're simply of people and worlds and war;
not the kind of war with armies,
the kind where self fights self,
sometimes using small words for big problems
and giant words for little problems.
Because who can say when a problem
is big or little
when it lurks solely in the mind?

The Dragon Tree

On a rock
far out in the ocean, sits
a tree.
Its trunk is
sturdy, like the
very rock itself.
And for good reason.
Instead of lush, flowing leaves adorning delicate branches that drift
to and fro
in the wind,
there are dragons.
Small, scaled balls of energy
with wings.
Their span is but a foot,
but the underside of those mighty beaters
shimmers like a plate of
mother-of-pearl.
Gripping the branches with
wrinkled, long-clawed toes,
the dragons feast on
tangy sap, ready to
take to the evening sky
for their task of catching the smokey, iridescent tears
of the moon
to fertilize the tree's hungry roots.

A Box Full of Kindling

You start by cross-dressing,
trying out every hat
and pant-suit
you can lay your snatching hands on.
Taking a nip
here and there
without even knowing,
pollinating the dry wood
with a peppering of ideas
and choosing to tempt
Pandora with the wild taste
of the unwritten.
An input always needs an output;
you present the light-child
who carries it.

Sunny Smiles

Buttermilk-stained plates
poke up from the fray
of earthy closeness.
They greet the day,
even if you don't want to,
and when you do, they'll be waiting
to gift you with smiles.

When the colour fades as the skies turn,
and the flesh huddles down
to protect itself from the oncoming
chill kisses,
you know that their solid will
is a promise
of their return.

Hullabaloo Bus

There was a wild bus
roaming the skinny streets of Shalfleet,
it wasn't enjoying its journey
so it decided to rest its wheeled feet.

Unfortunately it trapped its older brother
a short ways just behind,
the tamer had to get out
and direct the roaring traffic into a line.

But then the master came
and coaxed the beast to move.
On both brothers went
striding past the giant, backed up queue.

The Stasis of Soft-scaled Wings

Hanging around beneath the canopy,
your long, green dreadlocks
dangle in the air,
sucking the moisture away from the world.
As you drink, I see the life
return to your slender body,
the colour of your skin
ripens once more
and you rise up,
reaching for humid skies.
Your soft fingers remind me
of silver-white moths
floating on the breeze towards
the light splashing down
from the stars.

Between the Hour and the Minute

They tied themselves together, linking their hands with an elaborate wrap of solder. It was all for the dance; preparation for the endless twirling and spinning that was set to take place during the sixty seconds between midnight and one minute past. But that minute is never just a minute; to the right people, it is an eternity. They were the right people. They never came back.

Tillandsia and Cyanea

Today I saw the purple fairy
caress the garden's pink tongue.
She summoned her sister
and together they danced
among the long waterfall of grass
sweeping across the lands.

And then they vanished,
leaving only the fallen dust
of their violet wings.

I waited, my wonder
still clouding my eyes,
and I saw the ground
around the dust erupt,
sprouting forth twin pups.

Parking Ticket

Mind the clock
as the ticket-master
prepares to drop

the white leaf
onto the window;
a grim flash of teeth.

Upholding his duty.
The passenger inside flares
her nostrils at this cruelty

and in a flash of skirts
rises from her seat
to kick him where it hurts.

Printed Terrarium

Fingers run over silken leaves,
fertilizing inky seedlings,
nourishing them into vast trees
that bear glimpses
of future forests.
Hungry creatures,
ever wanting,
come to bathe amongst
these typeset giants,
absorbing rich worlds and ideas.
Terrariums of thought
and promise
dwell deep within,
rising up
when no words are left.
Bringing calm to the unpredictable,
chaotic, and often
unbearable web,
easing minds
as they wander barren plains.

Beauty Contest

How do you measure
the prettiness of a flower?
Do you look at it from every angle,
taking a ruler to each petal
and then recording the measurements
in order to conclude
perfect symmetry?
Do you lay them
next to others
of the same hue,
matching them with those
that have already won the vote
for overall vibrancy?
Do you gather them into a bunch
for an authority to assess
how well they can be displayed?
Or is it the case
that you do not judge them
at all?
Perhaps you have realised
that in order to fully observe
the beauty in each,
you must first appreciate
their differences.

A Painting of Venus

Opening up like a cracked
walnut shell
yearning to peek at the world,
you see a flash of blue satin
dance across the sky.
Tides rise high
and crash
with soft flecks
against your cheek,
staining your skin
with rainbows.
Under your feet
the earth shifts
to accommodate your scent.
It has known you
always,
but now
you have changed.
It must know you again.

The Shrouded House

Tucked away by a shroud
of blue-silver trees
is a house. Honeysuckle
clings to one side, sucking at the foundations,
and ivy to the other,
attempting the same, but
it is still too young to force
the bricks and mortar to crumble.
How old the house is, no-one quite knows,
and nobody wonders anymore.
It has simply always been,
part of the landscape of the sleepy village,
like the trees, the marsh, the hills
and the little creek that trickles
beside the gravel path.
Villagers move away and return,
families grow and people die.
The house watches it all,
making no comment except
to occasionally flap its shutters in the wind,
waving goodbye to old friends.

Part Three: Light on Water

A Message Without a Bottle

If I listen closely,
I can hear it.
Hear it in the swell,
in the foam,
in the salty droplets that land on my face,
even in the cries of the gulls
beating their white wings overhead.
The strong steady thrum
of distant lands
calling
calling
calling
rippling forever through the depths
like a record on repeat,
going around and around and around
until someone finally hears it
and lifts off the needle.
Message received.

Naked Reflection

In the mirror, I don't see myself. I see my plain face, worn eyes and body frame. (Summer: tabloids bleating 'beach body, beach body'. Pressure. Desperation. Hunger. Winter: recipe ideas that feed twelve guests. Temptation. Indulgence. Guilt.) But that's not actually *me*. This self doesn't exist in the mirror. In fact, I'm not even sure it exists at all anymore. I've been swallowed by a giant beast and squashed by everything else it consumes. I'm so far down that I can no longer see the light from its mouth. But perhaps there's still a chance that something in here can help me. I should start searching.

All That You See

My fingers do not work like yours,
but still I seem to type,
my hair falls out in clumps now
and my dark roots have all turned light.

It doesn't bother me
I'll wear it back, my friend,
or if that makes you uncomfortable
pretend it's a new fashion trend.

This is me, this is how I am
but the who that shines inside
cannot be defined by a disability,
even against your twisted pride.

Come now, don't be afraid
of a 'cripple' who talks back
and forces away all your expectations
to start you on a new track.

Oops, did I say something wrong?
Throw a spanner in the works?
Did I wipe away society's stereotypes?
I'll consider that a perk.

The Tufted 'Fro

The tall mast towers up
like a beacon
for the hungry-eyed,
proud as a parent lifting
their child onto their shoulders.
Strutting through the lanky,
overgrown forest,
the style turns many heads.
Citrus remarks are made,
but they don't wilt
your smile.

Who You Really Are

I want to climb to the stars,
feel the roar
of ovation in my ears.
Let euphoria take over
as my body balances
on the point of a needle
as it sways back and forth across the dial.
Precarious. Rash. Bold.
I am all these things.
As I wake,
I sink my hands
into my jarring heart
and replace the bent, broken cogs
with new ones.

Wear It On Your Heart

My hands fit right around your waist. I can pull you in tight, or let you go. We are sewn together, attached by a loose red string. You can wind it; so can I. Together, then. Hand over hand, gaze to gaze, we gather each other up into a tiny pin-badge pressed forever to our hearts.

Loud Voices

Overhead, the tannoy begins
its daily screech
calling on the broken people
to give up their reach.
Pulling the clouds back
across the brightening sky
and drumming in orders
mimicking the buzzing of a fly.
"Bring out the ear plugs,
let's deaden the sound!"
Someone shouts
circling the round.
At first, the response is dull,
little more than a whisper,
then the idea pops open
in their minds like a blister.
The movement surges,
a road is paved;
a future awaits where
they might all be saved.

The Direction of Melody

Sometimes a song catches in your head, going back and forth and around and around, like a wheel attached to a giant pendulum. It can lift you up, high enough to bring on fear but lose it at the same time, or it can bring you down, low enough to ground your feet for a moment and rest from the dizziness of the world. And sometimes it can leave you hovering in mid-air, giving you time to process everything up to that instant. That's when you have the chance to choose: up, or down?

Clouds with Wings

I stroll down the path,
well trodden, like the ones your feet
automatically follow even when you're not thinking where
you're going and suddenly find
a sharp turn;
you've arrived at your destination.
Yet this time,
I turn and find myself not
at the big, towering structure of work,
but stepping onto a white fluff
that spreads great feathered wings and lifts me up
high.
The wind whips my hair around,
obscuring my vision,
then it clears and I'm chasing dandelion seeds
across the skyline.

A V of birds passes nearby,
I wave at them,
wishing them luck in their new land.
My winged cloud plummets;
I wonder where it might stop.
It doesn't stop at all.
The ground rushes up, but I pass through it
into a dark, warm cocoon
of blankets and hot water bottles.
I realise I'm holding my breath.
I release it, along with my cosy shield
and find my feet
have stopped
right where they should.

To The Teacher Who Broke Me

There are certain days,
like those mornings just after a heavy downpour
where the scent of pollen and damp soil
mix to form that sickly, sweet smell,
and the sun comes out to create mocking shadows -
yes, days like those -
when nostalgia kicks in and I'm thrown
back to primary school,
clutching my satchel and walking into the playground
where all the other kids play without care
or squabble about nothing.

I sit on my own and watch.

Then the whistle blows
and she comes out, asking
us to line up.
A severe face carved
with severe eyes
and an even severer mouth,
but only when her gaze is turned to me.
Everyone else sees the smiling, caring mask
that tricks them into false security.
She speaks to them with soothing words,
but for me?
For me she leans in so that her severe face
is barely an inch from my own terrified one,
releasing the full roar of her lungs
into my ears.

I'm frightened.

I know she's watching me,
waiting for me to tell someone about her.
I try to hide it,
but soon the dread consumes me.
I am physically sick at the idea
of facing her again,
seeing the rage build up in her eyes
when I ask even a simple question.

My parents grow concerned.
They talk with her -
she gives them the smiling mask -
and when they leave,
she rounds on me,
raging on
until I am no smaller
than a pebble in her wake.

My face is wet.
I can't see;
I don't want to see.
A hand gently touches my shoulder:
it's time to speak up.
Tell them
what's really troubling you.
Tell them the truth
about her.

I do.

Three weeks later,
she is gone.
Never to return.

Her voice is still there
in my mind.

It's always there,
and so is the fear.

But now I can choose to ignore it.

Always Overhead

The umbrella looks down at me, taking in the shape of my head, the faint line of my hair parting and the curve of my neck as I stare at the puddle by my feet. In it, I can see the grey sky clearing. The umbrella's work is almost done. In fact, the light, misty drops that tickle its top are barely enough to worry about. Yet the umbrella is rooted to my hand. Perhaps, like I once needed it, it now needs me.

Spud Heart

Do you ever have those moments of delight
where something simple
yet unexpected happens?
Like when you think
you've harvested all the potatoes you planted,
only to be greeted the next year
by a fresh crop?
Or a plant you never knew
would flower
offers up delicate purple blooms overnight?
It's these little things,
these pure moments of joy
that present the chance
to see.

Roses are Green

There's a rose in the garden
without any buds.
No matter how much the gardeners try,
the rose turns away
and focuses on growing strong,
healthy green leaves
admired for being just that.
The rose has always known
flowering was not in its future.
And it's fine that way.

Open Your Eyes

Fire climbs up my flesh,
seeping through my pores -
my veins are charged
with impulse.
The ledge of the world is before me.
I step up and finally
see the vastness beyond.
Coiled, my knees spring
to launch
my body down.
I ride the air's waterfall;
I don't fear the fall.
Someone will catch me.
They always do.
And if that fails, my shoulders
will ignite with ember-flower wings
to carry me back
where I belong.

Dead Words

A tower of words merged into brick
waiting to crumble
like the decayed mast of a wrecked ship.

The alligators below all circle around
speaking of disaster and sacrifice
while they're safe on the ground.

An annual mania that ignores the dying,
green apologies are spoken;
they don't realise they're lying.

And then the opening buds of a rose
speak up with new voices
querying the world with new prose.

New

Pulling away the wasted,
darkened leaves;
limp limbs
both deprived of sustenance
yet fed too much;
l cast them out on the ocean
and watch them sink
below the surface.
Now the new growth can be seen
striving up towards the light.

Just Drifting

I have a little boat
made of brown,
overlapping leaves.
As it floats down the steady, gentle stream,
I lie back
and hook
my legs over the side
so my toes
kiss the cool water.
The movement makes a ripple.
The ripple knocks
against my little boat,
lulling me into a soft doze.
I walk in and out of dreams,
drifting along
enjoying the journey,
unconcerned by where
I might end up.
Just like my little boat,
edging on,
unconcerned,
down the stream.

Leaf Litter

Leaves drift across the way,
sweeping up the memories of
evening walks, lazy afternoon strolls and
those crisp morning jogs to catch the train.

Swirling up into a tight ball,
they cascade around my body
to fall at my feet.
I absorb them, as if they are a
soft mulch begging to fertilize.

A hundred rays of winter sun
swarm down to dance in my hair,
as the warm, soft rain
of spring drips onto my nose,
showering me with growth.

The rush of euphoria rides up my spine,
causing a clucking laughter to escape
my lips, jostling about on the humid breeze
to mingle with dawn's robust chorus.

A Book for Pandora

At the very bottom of the box, under all the aluminium ring-pulls, squashed bottle caps, tarnished costume jewellery, bent paperclips, and neat bags of lavender long lost of their scent, is a single book with one word stamped across its cover in gold lettering. The word looks familiar, but you can't recall what it means. You spell it out: H-O-P-E. The meaning refuses to stir in your mind, so you pick it up, turning it over in your hands and caressing the cover. A button catch clasps the book shut. Even when you press it, it refuses to open. Dismayed, and by now a little bored, you put the book back. Under the lavender bags, under the paperclips, under the jewellery, under the bottle caps and under the ring-pulls. Now the book is completely obscured, you close the lid of the box and turn away, intending to walk off and forget about it. But even though the book is hidden, buried under so much, you cannot let go of it. You know it's there, and it always will be there, waiting for you to pick it up again.

Part Four:
A Time, Once Upon

Ice on Lips

The splitting of the glass caused the earth
to cry out; caused the earth to cry out
with the agony of the darkest mottles
taking root in hearts and eyes,
framed into windows and tailored spectacles.
A vision of wrinkles, dark splotches cast
into marbled nature, now teach warped
learning to craft cunning thoughts.
Caught! The attention of ice, snowflakes
skitter down, plucking a kiss from
the lips of her cunning prey, wrapping
cool breath tightly about to mask
the journey through frozen skies.

Sprouted

Up, up.
Green shoots,
eager brown boots.
A steep climb
for a little crime:
coins here, coins there,
as jumpy as an adult hare.
For a good cause;
give yourself pause.
The goose's egg,
easily as big as your head,
a lilting harp
that never plays sharp.
Snatch them up quick!
Ears open, never miss a trick.
Down Down,
nearing the ground.
Run, lightning feet
through the patch of beet.
Safe for a while,
the end of the trial...

DOWN DOWN. DOWN DOWN.

Giant fists waiting to pound.

Uncovered

Why should my sensitivity
be a sign
of who I am?

Why
should I be measured by
the bruises I bear
from a night of unrest,
when all I asked for
was hospitality?

Why would you seek
to drug me
with pea-sized pills
and force me to climb
the innerspring tower,
when a simple question
would so easily give
rest to your doubts?

Don't take my truths
as acceptance
of your hand.

If you had
seen me
first, I may have reconsidered.

The cover has been
removed from you, not me.

Your chance has been spoiled:
blind

desire has that effect.
It coils within,
waiting for release.

Well-shaped Sand

Purple mist wisps down
shaded dunes, creeping hands
staining the yellow grains,
tumbling into bustling cities
ready to snatch at the wealth
of a merchant's wares:
sugared dates, pistachios,
beads and scarves and
a thousand other riches
to flavour sips of life.
Lit by the lamp's flicker,
illusions are stamped
over a tide of eyes,
but never reach the corners
filled with emptiness
bottled tightly into fancy glass.

A Shadow's Footsteps

The shadow of the second star
glides across creaking boards and
bloated sails, summoned by its youthful
keeper to sew it tight for the morn.
Safe from adults, hooked and
wigged, who pillage every source
for glittering trinkets and the dust
that brings spells of flight.
Yet twisted intentions hold no key,
only one power can grant the skies:
Belief.
From the full-lipped colours of
wild flowers, to the salt of deepest
seas, in the shimmer of a mermaid's
scale and the warmth of a firefly's glow
lies the echo of magic's pulse, keeping
the ever-grasping hands of Master
Time distant as dreams of rushing
hordes and striking clock towers.

To Question a Parent

What would you do
if your son grew crooked?
With crooked thoughts
and crooked ways,
gnarled and twisted
as a malformed tree?
Would you recognise him
if his roots were swept away
by time, humble origins replaced
by woven finery, declaring to
all who might listen
that his reputation at
spiriting away prized objects
has earned him the name
he always sought?
A Master, yes.
A legend among thieves.
Would you ask him
to prove his tremendous skill?
Would you care?
Or could you simply take
him back, proud that he
accomplished all he wished?
Would you say, 'My
Son is a man with
crooked thoughts and crooked ways,
yet never a body has he hurt.

He takes possessions,
but they are only such.
My son, the Master Thief.
We may be different,
but I am okay with that.'

A Temptation of Hair

It lay as a river
bathed in sunlight,
wrapped tight about
the stark tower
walls. A glistening
enchantment to entice
even the most self-controlled,
beckoning them up
to the draft-filled chamber.
Gold clad, she waits,
singing sweet nothings while
preparing to devour
their gossamer shrouded souls.

The Swan

Feathers leafed across
the opaline neck,
elongated by the sun's
dawn fingers. Reflections
change on the water's
surface; webbed feet
cracked into separate
toes.
Every night as moonface
greets the pale ripples,
a crown of moss
adorns the head,
mocking its gilded
cousin for the barrier
keeping them
apart.
A coarse voice soon
turns to music,
eased by lips instead
of beak. But the instance
is fleeting, a rolling
waiver shimmering with
the false promise of
escape.

Of Apples and Hearts

A weight of years until the apple seed grows,
wrapped in the anger of a thousand
wrongs,
yet once the tree matures and
swells with fat, succulent
globes,
the juice extracted is so sweet
that to savour it must surely
make it poison.
Polishing the red skin makes it glow
as vibrant as the dying
heart;
the white one takes a bite
cascading down to rest in a grave
of spirals.
But for all its power,
not even that can break the molten
hurt
residing in the chest of the gardener.

Rumpelstiltskin

Pointed, the spindle spins
weaving the golden thread that
gathers together all of humanity's desires.

The wheel rotates as the world rotates,
conjuring lustrous yellow
from dull.

But ever such beauty is poisoned
by greed,
the devious imp knows this.

Contorting knowledge to flay
unsuspecting beings, he languishes
in the sweet syrup of despair.

Laughing cowardly tears
as he drinks in the great
spoils of straw.

The One Who Owns the Rose

The sliding shriek of cutlery on fine bone china,
a cup falling down to chip on the hard stone.
Its pattern is ruined, but who cares?
It's just a cup.

The ticking of a clock on the mantelpiece
gathering dust until the particles clog its inner workings.
They grind to a halt, but who cares?
It's just a clock.

The candelabra placed on a table set for one,
its elegant white candles unburnt and dry.
Its golden finish is tarnished, but who cares?
It's just a candelabra.

The rose, cut so long ago from its bush,
each year its waxy, ruby petals fade even more.
They fall one by one, but who cares?
He does.

And now he panics.

Worn Shoes

Silver leaves fall
as the delicate slippers
pass, lightly tapping
through the long tunnel
bejewelled with diamond trees.
A shadow seeks
the fleeing twelve; invisible.
Gathering golden branches
and golden cups
to bring stone conclusion
before the blood majesty,
its weight weakens youthful
rows, but still does not
prevent the shoes
of evening grace
being danced through.

The Pulse of a Puppet's String

A heart of wood,
not easily turned,
yet crafted with
tides of love.
Resilient to all
afflictions, desiring
that which many dismiss:
humanity. Flesh.
The drumming of sanguine
rivers through a
blue-green maze,
a pillow inflated
with air inside
the kinetic cavity.
But porous grain
and rounded knots
only become sinewed
in the wake
of honesty and
its brother,
truth.

Arrow Play

A lover lost,
swept in by courtesy
and coin,
fine fabrics that glitter
as the deep divine.

A roguish grin
once jailed her heart
in petals,
a green-clad figure
both devious and kind.

A thief named,
hiding swift in shadow
and sight,
striving for his maid
to regain her Self.

A shattered laugh
embedded in his chest,
pointed wood
glued back into whole,
turgid with swollen hope.

Far Out in the Ocean

Dry, silver scales speak on my tongue
of glittering waves and the deepest depths.
But I can only reach them when
the blue calls me back.

When the blue calls me back and
the silver scales become me.
I long to dive down inside my mind
to search for the reason why;

I cannot recall ever being this hungry
for something my memory no longer holds.
Yet the pumping of my heart mirrors
the weight of liquid cornflowers.

And I know the foam will gather.
One day.

Through the Woods

I see you standing there,
my friend, waiting to
observe the one in red

riding through the woods
on a steed of illusion.
She gallops confidently

without care, oblivious
to the thud of hooves
disturbing their den.

You wish to protect her,
but why should you
expend such energy

for one who will never
know and never care
of your existence?

Concealed

In the forest
we'll hide the babe,
safe among the thorns,
but to raise her
kind of nature,
a price to pay we must
conform:
To give up all our
fairy dust, so those
curious of soul
won't turn our way and
turn this poor child's heart
black as toxic
coal.
We must turn our backs
on all we know
and learn afresh,
sweeping away
identity and sowing seeds
of happiness that
bless.

Mechanical Lungs

I gave you my voice
once. You had me
caught and caged,
ready to sing for
you and any audience.
To perform until my lungs
were spent, my fragile
frame shaking, but it made you happy;
I could see.
So I persevered, even though
my head would droop and my
light chest was gripped
with tightness.

Then you were gifted a metallic me.

It astounded you and every
beat
of
your
heart
was ensnared
by the grinding inner workings
as it chirped out
a charming replica of song.

You cast me aside,
I was free to fly again.
Free
to sing when I pleased or sing
not at all.

But eventually, as all things
do, the grinding of fake me
ground to a halt.
And your heart was released
to beat on its own.
The beat was weak.
You realised that it was starting
to break apart.
The cracks had appeared when you first
pushed me aside,
yet the pain was masked by false joy.

I can fix you,
bandage you up will warm trills
filled with spring flowers and
gentle breezes, the chorus of dusk and of dawn.
I can heal you.
If you ask.

Grey

If you're grey on the outside,
are you grey on the inside, too?

Forever a colour
that is not a colour?
Neither bright, nor dull
but a fluffy, half-formed
substance in-between?

A blur of identity,
an endless game of cat
and mouse,
see-sawing up and down,
with the fear of staying
who you are
at one end,
and the fear of
becoming someone new
at the other.

If you're grey on the inside,
are you grey on the outside, too?

Small Cares

Why do you hang your head
so low, my pet?
You may only be the size
of a snow drop or crocus,
and a puddle may appear
as a small lake to you,
but why is that a sad thing?
Think of all you can
see and hear
that no other can.
Observe the flowers as they first emerge,
seek the moment they reach for the sun!
See the bees buzzing back to their homes
and help them carry their bags of pollen.
Listen to the secrets of dormice
and ask to fly on the backs of butterflies.
Sleep in the shade of a snail's shell,
be carried by a team of worker ants.
But most of all, my pet: live!

The Long March

One, two, one two.

Line by line,
side by side,
up the steep mountain path
following the piper's march.

One, two, one, two.

Rock and stone,
wind and rain.
Soon we'll reach the river,
He doesn't care if we shiver.

One, two, one, two.

Unable to stop.
Unable to think.
Unable to breathe.

One, two, one, two.

All because the villagers;
our family, our kin;
refused to pay the price
that was owed
to him.

Said the Man to the King

Said the man to the King
(whilst concealing a grin):
Rolls of fabric, neat and trim
shroud your holy, pale skin.
Silver thread stitched thickly
around collar and sleeve, strictly
the finest for this work of art;
certainly, Sire, you'll look the part.
It's magic, I confess,
to help weed out those who are less
than intelligent at court,
it'll be a game, a sport,
for the dim witted cannot see
these garments made by me!

Said the King to the man
(though he was panicked by the plan,
for in fact he could not see
the clothes supposedly reaching his knees):
What cleverness, sir, you've shown,
I would truly never have known
that a charm could be used
to seek out those who have abused
their position by my side,
but now they cannot hide!

And so the next day,
to the townsfolk's dismay,
the King held a parade,
and a declaration he made
that any who claimed
his robes not to be, shamed
themselves and should admit
their serious lack of wit.
Yet among the mutterings
and unsure shuffling
a hum of laughter did climb
at the sight of the King's bare behind!

Pictures on the Hearth

Of glass slippers
and long carriage rides:
dreams are made
of soot.

But who shall
seek the owner
of the gleaming crystal's
foot?

Some say a prince,
tall and fair,
will search the long,
dark night.

Yet the wearer waits
not for a prince, but
a princess to come
in sight.

Together they will
cast aside stray
whispers of the
old.

Searching stars overhead
and gleaming lands
forgotten but long
foretold.

The Light that is Dark

In the night when the moon is high,
light brightens pale pebbles.
A guide to home.
Yet knowing home is
not where you're needed,
not where you're wanted,
not where you are even allowed to exist,
why do you still try to return?
Do you believe he will listen,
that your voices can override hers?
I know you want to believe in him.
But he was the one who left you here.

Dear reader,

We hope you enjoyed reading *A Book For Pandora*. Please take a moment to leave a review in Amazon, even if it's a short one. Your opinion is important to us.

Discover more books by Kathryn Rossati at https://www.nextchapter.pub/authors/kathryn-wells-fantasy-author

Want to know when one of our books is free or discounted for Kindle? Join the newsletter at http://eepurl.com/bqqB3H

Best regards,

Kathryn Rossati and the Next Chapter Team

You might also like:

Cancerwords by Ellyn Peirson

To read first chapter for free, head to:
https://www.nextchapter.pub/books/cancerwords

Lightning Source UK Ltd.
Milton Keynes UK
UKHW042008031220
374592UK00010B/731/J